A WALK WITH
JESUS
DOWN
HOPE
ROAD

**TRAVELING FROM BROKENNESS TO
HOPE ON THE ROAD TO EMMAUS**

MICHAEL MURRAY

Edited by Emily Lupfer

Scriptures are italicized and are taken from the following versions of the Bible:

THE HOLY BIBLE, NEW INTERNATIONAL VERSION®, NIV® Copyright © 1973, 1978, 1984, 2011 by Biblica, Inc.® Used by permission. All rights reserved worldwide.

The Holy Bible, New Living Translation (NLT), copyright © 1996, 2004, 2015 by Tyndale House Foundation. Used by permission of Tyndale House Publishers, Inc., Carol Stream, Illinois 60188. All rights reserved.

PHILLIPS MODERN ENGLISH BIBLE, by J. B. Phillips, "The New Testament in Modern English", Copyright© 1962 edition, published by HarperCollins.

The Common English Bible®, CEB® Copyright © 2010, 2011 by Common English Bible.™ Used by permission. All rights reserved worldwide.

Publishing services provided by  **Archangel Ink**

Paperback ISBN: 978-1-7379973-4-4

*To all who have suffered. To all
with unfulfilled hopes.*

*May we be reminded that our ultimate
hope is in the Man with the scars on
his body and holes in his wrists.*

Contents

Introduction:
"We Had Hoped..."

"We had hoped..."

Those might be the three most relatable words in all
the Bible.

Who hasn't hoped for something? And—maybe more
importantly—who hasn't been disappointed by a hope
gone unfulfilled?

A few months ago, I had my own run-in with disappointment. I was in the middle of writing the fourth
devotional book in my *Nobody Left Out* series. It was
going well, but then, without warning, I hit a wall and
crashed. I felt burnt out and overwhelmed.

At the same time, my family was facing some challenges.
My wife, Diana, struggles with chronic fatigue. And if
you've read any of my previous books, you may know
I have cerebral palsy, which presents another set of
issues. This makes caring for our wonderful two-year-
old son interesting. I have the energy, and Diana has

the coordination... *if only one of us could possess both at the same time!*

I decided to take a break from writing my book. Yes, sometimes writers need to grit their teeth and push through a tough spot. But there are other times when you need to set the book aside and rest. I sensed this was one of those times.

This doesn't only apply to writers, by the way. God calls all of us into seasons of rest. We may resist it because so much of our self-worth comes from being productive. I often feel a sense of guilt when I'm not getting "enough" done. (How much is "enough"? I don't know, but it's always *just a little more* than what I have already done!) These times of rest are a reminder that our value comes from who we are, not what we do. We are fully loved by God because we were created by him.

Over the next few weeks, my mind drifted to a Bible story that has always comforted me. It's a story about two people who love Jesus but are incredibly disappointed with life. It's a story that takes place on the first Easter Sunday. (But of course, they didn't know that then!) It's a story about hope, and I needed hope. And I knew I wasn't the only one.

The story is known as the Road to Emmaus. It's found in Luke 24:13-35. This account is one of the most beautiful portraits in Luke's gospel. It's also hilarious if you take a moment to imagine it. Two of Jesus' friends walk along a road, heartbroken that Jesus has died. *Then Jesus sneaks right up on them!* He joins them on their walk, but they don't recognize him. Slowly, though, hope returns to their hearts.

As I reflected on this story, I realized Jesus took these two disciples on a path of healing. The road they traveled had five different "mile markers." Jesus walked them through each one.

They began the day on **Broken Road**, feeling shattered by the tragic events they experienced that week.

Jesus then took them to **Disappointment Road**. Here, they got honest about their unfulfilled hopes.

Suffering Road was the next stop. This is where they found Jesus smack dab in the middle of their pain.

As they turned around a bend, Suffering Road gave way to **Redemption Road**. This is the part of the journey where they had to decide how to respond to tragedy and pain.

And then, surprisingly, the two disciples looked around and found themselves on **Hope Road**. But the hope they discovered wasn't the kind of hope you might expect. The hope Jesus leaves them with is a wounded hope. A hope marked by scars. And this is a deeper kind of hope than the world offers us.

It became clear to me that *this* was the book I needed to write at this moment in my life. Mostly because Jesus had something he wanted to teach me about hope. I wrote it over a period of 30 days. And looking back now, I can see how transformative those days were. Writing this book filled me with a new sense of hope. I pray it does the same for you.

In this short book, we're going to follow the same path the two disciples walked that first Easter morning. We will pass through those same mile markers, traveling from brokenness to hope on the Road to Emmaus.

There are five main chapters of this book. Each one looks at a small section of the Emmaus story. At the start of each chapter, I'll give you a passage of the Bible to read. Take a few minutes to read those verses before beginning the chapter. It will set the stage and provide context for what's to come.

All right, my friend, now go put on a comfortable pair of shoes!

It's time to take a walk with Jesus down Hope Road.

Michael Murray

Stop 1:
Broken Road

Bible Reading: Luke 23:44-24:16

Jesus called out with a loud voice, "Father, into your hands I commit my spirit." When he had said this, **he breathed his last**.

Our story begins on a sad Friday afternoon. But to Jesus' friends, it wasn't the beginning of a story. It was the end of one.

On that Friday afternoon, Jesus was brutally whipped, tortured, mocked, and hung on a cross to die. It was a slow, agonizing death. And if that wasn't enough, it was put on display like a carnival act. As people walked the busy streets of Jerusalem on Passover, they could stop to watch Jesus and two other men die a gruesome, inhumane death.

Finally, Jesus breathed his last breath. Maybe some in the crowd were relieved that Jesus was out of his misery after such a horrific day. It's a small consolation, but something, at least.

Yes, Jesus was dead. No one who was there that Friday could deny it. The sights, sounds, and smells of death were everywhere. How could things end this way?

Jesus was supposed to be like the star of every action movie. He was supposed to find a way to break free from that cross as heroic music swelled in the background. He was supposed to kick the butts of his enemies and save the day! But this time, the good guy lost. Scholar NT Wright describes it this way:

Jesus' followers believed he was not just a prophet, but the Messiah; and nobody expected the Messiah to die at the hands of the pagans. He was supposed to defeat them, not to succumb to their violence.[1]

And this is where our story begins: in brokenness and despair.

You know, I think God loves beginning new stories at sad endings. This might be where God does his best work! Of course, we can't see everything God is doing when we begin our walk down Broken Road. All we can see—all we can feel—is our pain.

Two days after this Bad Friday, a couple of Jesus' friends found themselves walking the dusty trail of Broken Road. Their journey is about to become ours.

---

1. Wright, N.T. *Luke for Everyone*. Westminster John Knox Press, 2004.

But before we join them, let's take a brief look at what happened between Friday and Sunday.

Mourning, Confusion, & Suppressed Hope

Jesus died a few hours before sundown, which marked the beginning of the Sabbath. There wasn't much time to give Jesus a proper burial, so a man named Joseph sprang into action. Somehow he convinced Pilate, the Roman governor, to release Jesus' body into his care. Joseph took the body, wrapped it up all mummy-like, and placed it in a tomb.

As a sidebar, there is so much more we can say about Joseph. Luke tells us he was a good man. He was also a member of the Sanhedrin—the group of religious leaders who handed Jesus over to Pilate. I am sure this made his life complicated as he struggled to navigate this situation. (This is also a good reminder that there were Pharisees and Jewish leaders who followed Jesus.)

In the end, Joseph did what he could to honor Jesus in death. He didn't want Jesus' body to be carelessly tossed into a pit. Matthew's gospel tells us the tomb was "Joseph's own new tomb that he had cut out of the rock" (Matthew 27:60). After placing Jesus' body inside, he rolled a ginormous stone in front of the tomb and scurried off to get home before sundown.

But Joseph was being followed! A group of women watched Joseph place Jesus' body in the tomb. The group included "Mary Magdalene, Joanna, [and] Mary the mother of James" (Luke 24:10). These women loved Jesus. They had witnessed the horror that unfolded that day. The Gospel of Mark tells us they "had followed [Jesus] and cared for his needs" (15:41).

Now that Jesus was dead, they wanted to do something to honor him, as Joseph had. So they hatched a plan: They would prepare some spices and perfume and anoint Jesus' body. (Because, as much as they appreciated Joseph's effort, they knew more needed to be done!)

They ran home and prepared everything. But since the next day was the Sabbath, they obeyed God's law and rested. What was the hurry, anyway? Jesus was dead, and dead bodies aren't going anywhere, are they?

I am sure Saturday was a day of despair for anyone who followed Jesus. Mourning mixed with confusion. Jesus rode into Jerusalem less than a week ago and seemed ready to take on the world. Now he is gone. It all happened too fast, and it still feels like a nightmarish blur.

When Sunday morning rolls around, the women resume their mission. They get up "very early in the morning" (24:1), probably because they hadn't slept a wink the night before. (If you've ever tossed and turned in your bed at night, Jesus' friends know how you feel.) The women pack up the spices and perfumes and make their way to the tomb. And that's when they get the shock of their lives!

They found the stone rolled away from the tomb, but when they entered, they did not find the body of the Lord Jesus. While they were wondering about this, suddenly two men in clothes that gleamed like lightning stood beside them. (Luke 24:2-4, NIV)

The women are bewildered, as any of us would be. But the men, who were angels, are bewildered by their bewilderment. "Why would you look for Jesus in a place where you put dead people?" they ask. "Jesus is alive!"

These women are the first people to hear the good news that Jesus is alive. It all seemed too impossible to be true. But then, somewhere in their minds, they remembered that Jesus had said something like this would happen. Still… *Dead people usually stay dead, right?* There was no time to process this right now. The women decide to make a mad dash back to home base and regroup with "the Eleven and all the others" (v. 9).

Who were these people?

The "Eleven" refers to the twelve men (minus Judas Iscariot) Jesus had chosen to work closely with him. They are the guys we usually call "the disciples." You know: John. Peter. Bart. (Yes, there was a disciple named Bart!) But Jesus had many other disciples, too. These are "the others"— women and men who loved and followed Jesus. And on this Sunday morning, they were all huddled together in a room, trying to make sense of what happened 48 hours earlier. Then, without warning, the door swings open, and the women burst in and deliver the news of what they saw.

But nobody believed their story of an empty tomb and two angels. Luke puts it bluntly: "They did not believe the women, because their words seemed to them like nonsense" (v. 11).

That's right. Nobody believed there was no body![2]

I can picture Thomas leaning against the back wall, arms folded. "Yeah, okay... And what did these two 'angels' look like? Hm? Hmmm??"

Peter can't believe it, either. But he's also impulsive and runs straight to the tomb to check things out for himself. When he arrives, he doesn't see the two men. But he doesn't see Jesus' body, either. All he finds are strips of linen. So he walks away, feeling more confused than ever.

---

2. As much as I'd like to take credit for this glorious pun, proper credit must be given to Pastor Andy Stanley.

Maybe a bit of hope did well up in Peter and the others when they heard the women's words. But hope can hurt when there's so much at stake. So they suppress it.

And this is where the story of the Road to Emmaus begins.

Moving On and Getting Over

What do you do when everything comes crashing down around you? How do you deal with the pain of a tragic event? You might try to put it behind you and move on with life the best you can. It's an approach I have attempted many times over the years.

John Mayer has a song called "Moving On and Getting Over," about trying to move on after a relationship goes south. But maybe we try moving on too quickly, before we've had time to process things. We can't help it. We want the pain to stop.

This is the place Jesus' friends found themselves that Sunday.

As morning turned to late afternoon, the excitement of the "empty tomb news" waned. A flame of hope rose up, but reality snuffed it out just as fast. There were more questions than answers. And, most importantly, one fact remained above all others: *Jesus was dead.* And so two of Jesus' disciples decide to "call it." They had enough. There's no reason to stick around any longer, so they pack up their belongings and hit the open road.

Now that same day two of them were going to a village called Emmaus, about seven miles from Jerusalem. They were talking with each other about everything that had happened. (Luke 24:13-14, NIV)

We don't know much about these two. Only one—Cleopas—is named. Some think they were husband and wife.[3] That makes sense to me because it appears they live together. But there's no way to know for sure. They could have been married, or they may have been related in some other way, perhaps siblings or cousins.

We also don't know why they were headed to Emmaus. Emmaus was seven miles from Jerusalem, about a two-and-a-half-hour walk. (Depending on speed, of course! It would probably be more like an eight-hour walk for me. Even longer if there were a Chick-Fil-A along the way. Then again, it was a Sunday, so no chicken biscuit break for me. *I digress...*) I think they lived in Emmaus and made the trip to Jerusalem for Passover. Now that things ended in disaster, why not go back home?

Whoever these two were, I find it strangely comforting that Luke doesn't give many details about them. It

3. Wright.

allows us to step into their shoes and experience the story for ourselves.

Maybe they met Jesus when he strolled through Emmaus one day. The crowds gathered to hear him speak, and these two people were amazed by what he said. Maybe he went to their home for dinner. Maybe he reminded them of how loved they were, no matter how messy or broken they felt. We don't know what their interaction with Jesus looked like. But we know they loved him.

This is a wonderful reminder that Jesus loves us all—not just the "rockstar" preachers and teachers. A lot of ink is spilled on Peter and John. Not so much on Cleopas and his companion. But they mattered to Jesus.

We might not know the name of the person who walked beside Cleopas. But Jesus did.

Jesus Walks Broken Road With Us

As the two travel, they begin discussing everything that happened over the past few days. Their thoughts wander back to the night Jesus was arrested. Chaos erupted throughout the city. No one knew what or who to believe. Things moved so fast, yet it all seemed like slow motion.

Their voices crack as they remember Jesus on that beam of wood. They can't get the sight of Jesus' lifeless, battered body out of their minds.

I am sure their grief felt like a two-ton weight. They may have been walking down the road to Emmaus, but to them, it was Broken Road.

And then, in the midst of their anguish, an unexpected stranger joins them. I love the way the CEB translation puts it:

While they were discussing these things, Jesus himself arrived and joined them on their journey. (Luke 24:15)

Notice what it doesn't say.

It doesn't say Jesus arrived and whisked them away from their pain.

It says Jesus arrived and *joined them* on their journey.

Jesus arrived in their brokenness and walked the road with them. And he does the same for us in our brokenness.

Isn't that beautiful? (I know, it's also frustrating because we would prefer the "whisk me away from pain" option!)

Luke also says, "they were kept from recognizing him"

(v. 16). But why? Why wouldn't Jesus just say, "Hey guys, guess what? It's me! I really am alive! Now let's get back to Jerusalem and open our Easter baskets before Bart eats all the peeps!"

That would have been more convenient and saved a lot of time. But Jesus isn't primarily concerned about convenience. He wants to teach these two people he loves something about hope. And sometimes, discovering hope takes time. There are no shortcuts because, like any good road trip movie, it's about who we become along the way.

So, for now, Jesus quietly joins them on their journey. As they walk the road, they will begin to open up about their brokenness. Things didn't turn out the way they hoped. Their world is spinning out of control. They're not sure which way to go from here. And Jesus listens.

There is one more thing I would like us to see in these first few verses of the story. Our two friends had Jesus to walk Broken Road with them. But they also had each other.

Pain can prevent us from seeing how God is working in our life. That is why it is so important to be in community.

When I look back on sad times in my life, I remember

15

the people who came alongside me. The people who sat by me as I cried. The people who reminded me that God was still good, and I was loved by him. Sometimes it felt like they were carrying me down the road.

Invite people you trust to walk Broken Road with you. And join others in their walk. It's a two-way road!

Admitting that things are broken is the first step toward hope. When we acknowledge the brokenness in the world (and ourselves), we can be honest with God about our disappointments.

Next stop: Disappointment Road.

💬 *Questions to Ponder:*

How do you deal with tragedy and despair when it hits you? Have you ever tried "moving on with life" before you've had the chance to grieve?

What are your thoughts on who Cleopas and his companion were? Why do you think they were headed to Emmaus?

Have you ever compared yourself to a "rockstar" Christian? How does it feel to know Jesus knows you by name and loves you?

Who has walked with you down Broken Road? Is there anyone you can come alongside as they walk down Broken Road?

Before we move on to the next stop, take some time to grieve what's broken in:

the world,
your life,
and you.

Stop 2:
Disappointment Road

Bible Reading: Luke 24:17-24
Supporting Passages: 2 Corinthians 7:2-7; Luke 9:18-27

*"The chief priests and our rulers handed him over to be sentenced to death, and they crucified him; **but we had hoped** that he was the one who was going to redeem Israel."*

It's difficult for Christians to be honest with God about their disappointments.

We know God is good, and we are grateful for all his provisions. But when tragedy strikes, we struggle to express our true feelings to him. It's almost as if we feel the need to protect his reputation. So we throw out platitudes like, "God is in control" and "It's all part of his plan." (And yes, God *is* in control, and he *does* have a plan. But that doesn't mean we need to stuff down our pain and just put on a happy face.)

I think a lot of our disappointment with God comes

from misplaced expectations. Some of us were told that if we behave enough, blessings will pour down, and we'll have an amazing life full of victories. So we tried our best to "be good." But we still face disappointments in life.

The Napoleon Dynamite Effect

Remember the movie *Napoleon Dynamite*?

I was in college when it came out, and the buzz around campus was that it was the funniest movie ever. I didn't get to see it in theaters. But months later, it was still the talk of the town. People were amazed I hadn't seen it yet. How could I miss the comedic event of the century? (The century was only four years old at that point, but still...)

I finally rented it on Netflix. I couldn't wait to watch it. (Back in those days, you had to wait for them to ship you a DVD! *I'm such an old man...*) Based on what I'd heard, I expected to keel over in laughter. I hit the "play" button and waited for my life to change forever.

Two hours later, I sat in silent disappointment.

That's it? I thought.

Now, if you love *Napoleon Dynamite*, don't worry. I think

it's a fun flick. The problem wasn't so much the movie but my expectations of it. I had visions of rolling on the floor, sides aching from my fit of laughter. When reality didn't match those expectations, the movie became one giant letdown.

Jesus' friends were sad that he died. They lost someone they loved. But what made Jesus' death all the more crushing was the expectations they had placed on him. We will explore those misplaced expectations toward the end of this chapter. But first, let's rejoin our friends along the road.

The Gift of Space

When we last left Cleopas and his companion, they were walking the road to Emmaus with Jesus. But they had no idea it was him. As he did so many times before, Jesus asks a question to invite conversation:

[Jesus] asked them, "What are you discussing together as you walk along?" They stood still, their faces downcast. (Luke 24:17, NIV)

"Tell me what's going on, guys," Jesus says.

At first, their pain is so deep they can't even muster up a response. All they can do is stand there with gloomy faces.

I think it's interesting that Luke uses the word "downcast" to describe their spirits. In 2 Corinthians, Paul tells us God "comforts the downcast" (7:6). Isn't that a beautiful picture of what's happening here? These two disciples are downcast, and Jesus is right by their side! Being a Christian doesn't mean we're always happy. It means we can embrace sadness, knowing Jesus is in it with us.

After a few moments pass, Cleopas responds:

One of them, named Cleopas, asked him, "Are you the only one visiting Jerusalem who does not know the things that have happened there in these days?" (v. 18)

Cleopas is amazed that this mystery man doesn't know about all the drama that went down in Jerusalem. Jesus' arrest and crucifixion was a spectacle. Had this strange guy been hiding under a rock? (No, but he had been hiding *in* a rock!)

Of course Jesus knows what's been going on. He knows their pain and why they are sad. But rather than jumping in to fix everything, Jesus gives them space to share what's on their hearts.

"What things?" [Jesus] asked. (v. 19)

In other words, "Tell me what grieves you. Share your disappointments with me as we walk down the road."

I think we can learn something profound from Jesus in this moment. When we encounter people who are sad, our first reaction might be to cheer them up. It makes sense. We love them and don't want to see them in pain. But maybe the best gift we can give someone who's grieving is space. Not physical space, but the space for them to honestly talk about their disappointments. That can be uncomfortable. Being in the presence of pain is not a pretty sight. But it is holy ground.

And when dealing with our own disappointments, the most courageous thing we can do is share them with someone else. It takes vulnerability to let people see our pain. But the people around us—the people who love us—won't know what is going on until we tell them.

"We Had Hoped"

After Jesus gives his two friends space to process, it's like the floodgates open. It's incredible what people will share when they feel safe enough to do so. I imagine the two of them talking over each other as they say the following:

"About Jesus of Nazareth," they replied. "He was a prophet, powerful in word and deed before God and all the people. The

22

chief priests and our rulers handed him over to be sentenced to death, and they crucified him; but we had hoped that he was the one who was going to redeem Israel. And what is more, it is the third day since all this took place." (Luke 24:19–21, NIV)

The two give a succinct summary of the ministry of Jesus. He had said and done amazing things. When Jesus was around, it felt like anything was possible. The energy in the air was electrifying! But then, in the span of one day, everything came crashing down. Jesus was arrested and crucified.

Then they utter my three favorite words of this passage. They are the words that drew me into this story so many years ago. And even now, they won't let me go.

"We had hoped."

They are so honest about their disappointment.

They had hoped Jesus would be the one to redeem Israel. But instead, he died a criminal's death, and it devastated them.

What about you? What did you hope for that didn't turn out the way you expected?

I had hoped she would come back.

23

I had hoped he would break off the affair and stay committed to me.

I had hoped I would finally get that promotion at work.

I had hoped the kids would drop by to visit more often.

I had hoped the cancer was gone for good.

I had hoped he would quit drinking.

I had hoped my second marriage would be better than the first.

I had hoped my relationship with my family wouldn't be so dysfunctional.

I had hoped the church would accept me as I am.

I had hoped to do more in life.

There are an infinite number of "I had hoped..." scenarios. They come in all shapes and sizes and are as varied as we are. But they have one thing in common: They are hard to say out loud because it feels like admitting defeat.

I admire the courage Cleopas and his companion had to share their disappointment. You can feel their weariness. Every last drop of hope has been wrung out of them.

After talking about Jesus' death, they switch gears to another topic: the strange events of that morning. It's like they're verbally processing what happened. They discuss the women finding the empty tomb. There were rumors of angels who said Jesus was alive. Then, they cap it off with this remarkable statement:

"Some of our men ran out to see, and sure enough, his body was gone, just as the women had said." (v. 24, NLT)

Imagine that! They know the tomb is empty. They know there are rumors Jesus is alive. But still, they dare not hope. They dare not allow themselves to "go there." It would be much too painful if it turned out to be a hoax. So they cut their losses and head for home.

Disappointment has the power to make us never want to hope again. And yet, the only way back to Hope Road is to be honest about those disappointments.

A Shift in Perspective

The disappointment Jesus' friends felt was real. But it's also true that they stemmed from misplaced expectations. The disciples had their own "Napoleon Dynamite" moment.

They had hoped Jesus would be the one to redeem Israel. That's not a bad hope to have! But they thought they knew what that redemption would look like. When it didn't happen the way they thought it should, their whole world turned upside down.

During that time, the nation of Israel was under Roman rule. And the Roman government took advantage of every opportunity to flex its power. Public crucifixion was just one ghastly reminder of who was in charge. Roman soldiers could also force Jewish people to carry their gear for one mile (something Jesus famously comments on in Matthew 5:41).

Naturally, Israel wanted to break free from Rome's oppression. They longed for the day when God would set things right and rescue them. And this expectation wasn't without precedence. A couple of centuries earlier, a group called the Maccabees led a successful revolt against the Seleucid Empire's hold on Israel.

When Jesus rode into Jerusalem on Palm Sunday, the disciples thought this was *their* moment of liberation. They saw Jesus as the one who would defeat their enemies.[4] He had to be the one they'd been waiting for.

---

4. Stein, Robert H. *The New American Commentary: Luke*, Broadman Press, Nashville, TN, 1992, p. 611.

And then, by the end of the week, it all went up in flames. Rome had squashed Jesus like a bug.

"This is what happens when you go up against Rome!" said the cross loud and clear.

This is why Jesus' friends are so disappointed. They had a vision of how the story would play out. Jesus would teach the bad guys a lesson. When that didn't happen, they were devastated.

The irony, of course, is Jesus *did* redeem Israel. He just didn't do it in the way his friends expected. He chose the path of suffering over the path of power. As NT Wright points out:

Cleopas's puzzled statement only needs the slightest twist to turn it into a joyful statement of early Christian faith: 'They crucified him – but we had hoped he would redeem Israel' would shortly become, 'They crucified him – and that was how he did *redeem Israel.*[5]

It was hard for the disciples to picture a scenario where God would allow Jesus to suffer. But Jesus alluded to it many times. Earlier in Luke, he basically spelled out the whole plan!

And [Jesus] said, "The Son of Man must suffer many things

---

5. Wright.

and be rejected by the elders, the chief priests and the teachers of the law, and he must be killed and on the third day be raised to life." (9:22, NIV)

I can't judge Jesus' friends for wanting victory without suffering. I want that too! And too often, that is the narrative we have been given in Christianity (especially American Christianity). If we just believe the right things, read the Bible, go to church, and vote for the right person, we'll avoid suffering. And when we do all those things and still face disappointments, we feel like the disciples on the road. We are crushed.

But the good news is Jesus walks Disappointment Road with us. Even when our disappointments come from misplaced expectations, he knows they are no less real. And as we walk the road together, he invites us to see our story from a different perspective.

Admitting our disappointments is the second step toward hope. When we acknowledge our disappointments, we can begin to embrace suffering with Jesus by our side.

Next stop: Suffering Road.

💬 *Questions to Ponder:*

Have you ever experienced the "Napoleon Dynamite Effect," where your expectations for something turned out different from reality? How did you deal with the letdown?

How have you seen God comfort you when you have been "downcast"?

When you encounter someone who is sad, how do you normally respond? How can you create a safe space for others to share their disappointments? (And when they do open up and share, how can you thank them for being courageous and trusting you with part of their story?)

What did Jesus' disciples hope Jesus would do? How did he go against their expectations?

Have you ever encountered a version of Christianity that promised X if you did Y? How did it affect your relationship with God?

What is a hope you had that didn't turn out the way you expected? Who can you share your disappointment with?

Before moving on to the next stop, take some time to grieve your disappointments as you share them with Jesus.

Stop 3:
Suffering Road

Bible Reading: Luke 24:25-27
Supporting Passages: Colossians 1:15-23; 2
Corinthians 4:1-12

*"Wasn't it clearly predicted that the Messiah **would have
to suffer** all these things before entering his glory?"*

There is a scene in *The Wizard of Oz* where Dorothy and
her friends wander down a dark road. They are heading
to the Wicked Witch's castle in an attempt to obtain her
broomstick. The Lion comes across a sign and reads
it: "I'd turn back if I were you!" He nods in agreement
and begins to turn around. Luckily, the Scarecrow and
Tin Man intervene and keep him on course.

We are about to step foot on Suffering Road. It's a part
of this journey I don't like at all. I want to turn back
around like the Lion. But that's why we need other
people to walk with us. So let's stick together, okay?
Because if we make it through, hope is waiting around
the bend.

The Stranger Speaks Up

When we last left Cleopas and his companion on the road, they had unloaded their burdens on Jesus (who they still think is a stranger). They expressed their disappointment and sadness over the events that had taken place the past few days.

Up until now, Jesus has been mostly silent. All he's done is ask a couple of questions, allowing his friends to express how they felt. But now, the stranger speaks up:

He said to them, "How foolish you are, and how slow to believe all that the prophets have spoken! Did not the Messiah have to suffer these things and then enter his glory?" (Luke 24:25–26, NIV)

Whoa! Jesus is bringing the heat!

His words seem abrupt, don't they? But I don't think they come from a place of anger. I think Jesus wanted these two disciples—who he loved deeply—to open their eyes. He wanted them to remember the cross was always meant to be part of the story.

Jesus' disciples had their hope in the wrong thing. They wanted glory without suffering. But Jesus' plan was to achieve glory *through* suffering.

The "How Could God Allow Suffering?" Dilemma

It's not a surprise that one of the biggest objections to Christianity (and God in general) is the state of the world. Look around. There's pain, disease, wars, famine. How could God allow all that suffering?

One morning I woke up to a series of not-so-friendly comments on one of my Facebook posts. They were all by one guy, and he was ridiculing me for believing in a God who would allow such heinous things to happen.

I have to admit—he made his point well. He started posting images of disabled and starving children. I believe in a God who allowed *that*?

He wouldn't let up, and I barely had time to respond to one comment before he posted another. But underneath all his anger, I could see his pain. He had a deep sense that the world was not as it should be. *And he was right!*

But here's the thing: God never promised us a life free from suffering. Other people may have sold us that idea and tried to pass it off as Christianity. But it is not an accurate picture of the Christian worldview. The pages of the Bible remind us we are living outside Eden— outside of the life God longs for us to have.

This is a silly example, but I am a fan of musicals, so let's try it: Imagine you go to see a musical. When it's over, you exit the theater with a specific complaint. "I can't believe the characters in that play were singing songs! How could they call that a musical?!"

That would be a bit odd, wouldn't it?

Now, you might not *like* when characters in a play break out in song every ten minutes. But if you buy a ticket to see a musical, you shouldn't be *surprised* by it.

My point is this: We may not like it, but we shouldn't be surprised by suffering, *especially* if we follow Jesus. We know how messy the world is. We know how messy we are. We have broken the peace we have with God, others, and even ourselves.

True Christianity doesn't say we can avoid suffering if we follow Jesus. It says Jesus entered into this world to experience suffering *with us*. And because he defeated death on the cross, we can look forward to the death of suffering. (As well as the death of death itself!) But even as we await that beautiful day, we're invited to join Jesus in the work of setting things right *now*.

Have we bought into a story that denies suffering?

If we have, we need to go back to the cross. It was

always part of the plan. As we saw in the last chapter, Jesus spoke about it many times. And the night before he was crucified, Jesus warned that we wouldn't be exempt from suffering, either:

"I have told you these things, so that in me you may have peace. In this world you will have trouble. But take heart! I have overcome the world." (John 16:33, NIV)

I'm not saying this makes going through suffering any easier. And it doesn't mean we should shrug our shoulders at suffering, either. Quite the opposite! Because Jesus entered our mess, we can enter the mess of others.

One of my favorite podcasts is The Pastor's Table. In each episode, a pastor shares their insight into the struggles of doing ministry.

In one episode, Pastor Rob Prince shared a story about a member of his church who was dying of cancer. She had no nearby family, so he and his wife welcomed her into their home. They took care of her, and she stayed with them until her death. It was sad to see her grow weaker each day, but they did what they could to alleviate her pain.

At the end of the episode, one of the hosts said this:

That's the power of the gospel. We're not afraid to enter into those dark places. We're not afraid to be with those who are suffering.[6]

My Facebook friend wasn't wrong to point out all the horrific things in this world. The anger we feel when we encounter suffering reflects God's desire to set things right. It's an invitation to join God in bringing his kingdom to earth as it is in heaven. The call of the Christian isn't to ignore suffering or explain it away. It's to join in the fight against it.

Honoring Josh's Journey Down Suffering Road

As I began writing this chapter, my friend Josh kept coming up in my mind. I want to share some of his story.

I met Josh in second grade. We were both in a classroom with kids who had a wide variety of disabilities. Josh had muscular dystrophy, a terrible disease that causes your muscles to deteriorate. The speed varies, but over time the body grows weaker. The life expectancy for a child with muscular dystrophy is around the age of 16 to early 20s.

When I first met Josh, he was able to walk. Sometimes he would push me in a wheelchair if we had to travel across campus for an event. (I can walk but tire out quickly if going a long distance.) He was soft-spoken but quick-witted. He had a talent for drawing and was in art club. He'd always be doodling during class (and would often get scolded by the teacher for it!).

I knew Josh throughout the rest of elementary and middle school. I watched his body grow weaker. After a couple of years, he was in a wheelchair but was able to push himself. Shortly after, he needed an electric wheelchair because his arms became too weak.

By eighth grade, he could no longer lift his arms. Though it was a struggle, he could still move his hands, which allowed him to continue his hobby of drawing.

It was sad to watch MD take over Josh's body. At the same time, I don't think I fully recognized how horrible it was. We never spoke about it. I wish I knew what Josh was dealing with on an emotional level. I wish I had asked.

We went to different high schools and soon lost touch. But toward the end of my sophomore year, I got word that Josh had passed away.

My parents and I attended the funeral, and I learned some things I never knew about Josh. His parents spoke about Josh's relationship with God. It became evident that Jesus walked with Josh through his suffering.

I want to honor Josh's journey down Suffering Road. I don't want to dismiss it with phrases like, "At least he's in a better place now" (however well-intentioned they may be). Even though it hurts, I want to look his suffering square in the eye. Yes, Jesus was with Josh, but that didn't make the pain any less real. It didn't make the disease he succumbed to any less cruel. And yet, I also look forward to the day when God's kingdom is fully realized on earth, and I see my friend again.

Maybe the best way to honor suffering—our own and others'—is to:

1. acknowledge that it's real;
2. accept God's invitation to do what we can to alleviate it in the now;
3. and look forward to the beautiful day when Jesus puts it in its grave.

Jesus Doesn't Abandon Us

I'm beginning to think it was a fool's errand to try to tackle the topic of suffering in one chapter of a short book. There is so much more to say! Entire volumes have been written about it by people way smarter than me. If you're interested in exploring it further, one book I recommend (especially in our current culture) is *On Getting Out of Bed: The Burden and Gift of Living* by Alan Noble. Two other great books on the topic are *Walking with God through Pain and Suffering* by Timothy Keller and C. S. Lewis's classic *The Problem of Pain.*

The message I want to convey here is that Jesus doesn't abandon us when we get to Suffering Road. He continues the journey with us. Let's return to our two friends on the road for a moment.

After Jesus reminds them that the Messiah had to suffer, what does he do next? He draws closer to them:

And beginning with Moses and all the Prophets, he explained to them what was said in all the Scriptures concerning himself. (Luke 24:27, NIV)

As they walked the next few miles toward Emmaus, Jesus talked through the Hebrew scriptures with them.

Imagine that conversation! If only we could be a fly on the head of Cleopas...

Jesus goes through God's big story and reveals how it all points to him. As it says in the book of Colossians, "He is before all things, and in him all things hold together" (1:17, NIV).

We may have a million questions about suffering, and asking those questions is okay. But we can be sure of one thing: Jesus holds us together in the middle of the mess.

As we close this chapter, I want to look at some words from the apostle Paul. Paul's life is proof that following Jesus doesn't mean we are exempt from suffering. Paul's life got harder the day he crossed paths with Jesus! But as he reflected on his sufferings, he wrote these words:

We are pressed on every side by troubles, but we are not crushed. We are perplexed, but not driven to despair. We are hunted down, but never abandoned by God. We get knocked down, but we are not destroyed. Through suffering, our bodies continue to share in the death of Jesus so that the life of Jesus may also be seen in our bodies. (2 Corinthians 4:8–10, NLT)

Honoring the suffering in this world is the third step toward hope. When we embrace suffering with Jesus by our side, the door to redemption swings wide open.

Next stop: Redemption Road.

💬 *Questions to Ponder:*

What do you think of Jesus' response to Cleopas and his companion (v. 25–26)? Why was it so important to him that they remember suffering was part of the plan all along?

Have you ever questioned God's existence (or goodness) because of suffering? Have you ever encountered a version of Christianity that promised "all glory and no suffering"?

Have you ever been tempted to try to "explain away suffering"? How can you join in the fight against it instead?

How have you seen or felt Jesus draw close to you in times of suffering?

In this chapter, we discussed three ways to honor suffering. (Acknowledge that it's real, accept God's invitation to alleviate it in the now, and look forward to the beautiful day when Jesus puts it in its grave.) Who do you know that is suffering right now? How can you honor their suffering?

What suffering are you experiencing right now? How can you honor your suffering?

Before moving on to the next stop, take some time to acknowledge the very real suffering in the world, both in your life and the lives of others. Allow yourself to feel any emotion it brings up— sadness, anger, fear, doubt, anxiety, etc. Let Jesus know how you feel.

Stop 4:
Redemption Road

Bible Reading: Luke 24:28-31
Supporting Passages: Mark 9:2-29; Luke 22:14-19

*Suddenly, their eyes were opened, and **they recognized him**. And at that moment he disappeared!*

We have turned a corner on our journey. The sun is peeking through the clouds ever so slightly. Take a deep breath of the sweet air and look around.

Hope is in the distance!

It may seem counterintuitive that we must pass through Suffering Road to get to hope. But if suffering weren't a reality, we wouldn't need hope. People who have perfect lives have no use for it. But for those of us in the middle of the mess, hope is what keeps us going. And so, onward we go!

When we last left our friends on the road, they were

having an epic Bible study with Jesus. He explained that a suffering Messiah was always part of the plan. The walk from Jerusalem to Emmaus would take about two hours. I wonder if time stood still for Cleopas and his companion as Jesus taught them. And remember, at this point, they still think he is some random guy who joined them on their walk!

Being With Jesus Is Like Being Home

Soon, the two disciples look around and realize they have arrived in Emmaus. Where did the past few hours go? The sun has already started setting, but they don't want their time with this stranger to end. So they invite him into their home.

As they approached the village to which they were going, Jesus continued on as if he were going farther. But they urged him strongly, "Stay with us, for it is nearly evening; the day is almost over." So he went in to stay with them. (Luke 24:28– 29, NIV)

Whoever this mystery man is, he has lifted their spirits. His presence has made them braver, and they feel they can carry on with him by their side.

I've been watching a lot of *Finding Nemo* with my two-year-old son recently. Toward the end of the movie, Nemo's dad, Marlin, wants to part ways with Dory.

43

Dory has short-term memory loss but has gained confidence with Marlin by her side. She says these beautiful words about how she remembers things better when he's around:

It's there. I know it is because when I look at you, I can feel it. And I, I look at you and... I'm home.

No matter how many times I've watched that scene, it's a struggle not to burst into tears.

If we spend a little time with Jesus, we won't want to be anywhere else.

A Meal to Remember

After Jesus enters their home, he shares a meal with them:

When he was at the table with them, he took bread, gave thanks, broke it and began to give it to them. (24:30, NIV)

Many commentators have pointed out the similarity between this meal and the Last Supper[7]. Luke uses the same language to describe it. At that meal, shared with the Twelve the night before his crucifixion, Jesus also "took bread, gave thanks and broke it, and gave it to them" (Luke 22:19, NIV).

---

7. Stein, p. 613.

Cleopas and his companion weren't at that meal four days ago. But now Jesus is reenacting it for them. That night, he told his friends his body would be broken for them. And now, as the two take the bread, something amazing happens:

Then their eyes were opened and they recognized him, and he disappeared from their sight. (v. 31, **NIV**)

Whaaaat?!

This is where our story turns from tragedy to comedy.

As they take the bread and begin to take a bite, they glance at the stranger and get the most wonderful shock of their lives. This man they've traveled with is none other than their friend Jesus! In the middle of their darkest hour, Hope was right there in front of them. They just couldn't see it.

Take a minute to read verses 30–31 again, and visualize it in your mind. I bet it will be tough to hold back a smile. You might even find yourself laughing! These little moments of redemption are why I love the Bible so much.

I imagine both of them spitting the bread out of their mouths as they recognize Jesus. They begin sputtering, trying to find the words to say. But before they can make a sound, Jesus has vanished from their sight.

I think it's beautiful that God opens their eyes after Jesus gives them the bread. They had spent the past couple of hours learning about how Jesus had to suffer. Now they are given a tangible reminder of Jesus' broken body.

It seems they can only recognize Jesus when they accept that suffering is part of his story.

It was a meal they would never forget.

Doing the Next Right Thing

Cleopas and his companion recognized Jesus was with them in the middle of their pain. That revelation sent them down the path of Redemption Road. In the next chapter, we'll see how their story ends. But for the rest of this chapter, I want to explore what redemption might look like in our lives.

I think redemption begins when we have the courage to do the next right thing even when all seems lost. It's taking a step toward Jesus in the darkness, even when we doubt he's there to catch us. It's living as if the story of Jesus were real, even when we can't muster enough faith to believe it. It's crying out, "I do believe; help me overcome my unbelief!" like the sick boy's father did in Mark 9.

My favorite book in the Chronicles of Narnia series

is *The Silver Chair*. It has my favorite character, a "Marshwiggle" named Puddleglum. Puddleglum is as gloomy as his name sounds. He always points out the worst possible outcome in every situation. <u>And yet, he is always willing to do the next right thing, even when he doesn't think it will do any good.</u>

In one scene, Puddleglum and his friends try to rescue Prince Rilian from the evil Queen. The Queen has thrown a magical powder into the fireplace, and the smell is making them drowsy. Under this trance, the Queen is able to get them to doubt everything they know to be true. Soon, they are questioning the very existence of Aslan (the Jesus figure throughout the books). All hope is lost. But then Puddleglum gathers the courage to take one step into the literal fire:

The Prince and the two children were standing with their heads hung down, their cheeks flushed, their eyes half closed; the strength all gone from them; the enchantment almost complete. But Puddleglum, desperately gathering all his strength, walked over to the fire. Then he did a very brave thing. He knew it wouldn't hurt him quite as much as it would hurt a human; for his feet (which were bare) were webbed and hard and coldblooded like a duck's. But he knew it would hurt him badly enough; and so it did. With his bare foot he stamped on the fire, grinding a large part of it into ashes on the flat hearth.[8]

---

8. Lewis, C.S. *The Silver Chair*. HarperCollins, 1953.

I love the bravery of Puddleglum. He does the next right thing, even when he doesn't know how it will end. But what I find more amazing is what happens next.

With the fire out, the Queen's power over her prisoners is broken. But a cloud of doubt still hangs over Puddleglum. He still can't be sure what he believes. But then he utters these words:

I'm on Aslan's side even if there isn't any Aslan to lead it. I'm going to live as like a Narnian as I can even if there isn't any Narnia.

These are beautiful and profound words. When we find ourselves on Broken, Disappointment, and Suffering Road, it's hard to see two feet in front of us. We stumble along, grasping for a hand to hold. We doubt God is good, and that is okay. In describing how God sometimes feels absent, theologian Mike Bird has said, "Sometimes Jesus sits with you in a dark room and you don't know it until he turns the lights on."[9]

If your faith is hanging by a thread, you're in good company. None of Jesus' friends had faith that first Easter morning. Hope seemed so far away. And if that's where you find yourself right now, I've been there too. Many times.

---

9. Bird, Michael F. *Divine Absence and Divine Comedy*, michaelfbird. substack.com/p/divine-absence-and-divine-comedy.

My encouragement to all of us going through hard times is to lean into the story of Jesus. Let's dare to live as if it were true, even when we can't see that it is. Because when we do, we might look up and find that Jesus has been walking the road with us the whole time.

Small Steps

I find it interesting that Jesus did not force his way into the disciples' home. When they arrived in Emmaus, they could have told him, "Well, you've said some fascinating stuff. But Jesus is still dead, and nothing will change that. So please stop talking nonsense. Goodnight, and good luck to you."

But instead, they felt a nudge to invite this stranger into their home for dinner. And they followed it without knowing what would come next. This small act brought them one step closer to redemption.

In 2009, an American exchange student in Italy named Amanda Knox was put on trial for murdering her roommate. Although there wasn't a shred of evidence against her, she was found guilty. By that time, Amanda had already spent two years in prison. In 2011, her conviction was finally overturned. She was released after four long years.

During her time in prison, there was no redemption in

sight. She was wandering deep down Suffering Road. She began to ask herself, *How do I make my current reality a life worth living?* This was her answer:

*That was a big question, one I couldn't answer in its grandest sense. But there was a smaller version of that question: how can I make my life worth living **today**? I could answer that. That was entirely in my power. So I did that. Doing sit-ups, walking laps, writing a letter, reading a book—these things were enough to make a day worth living. I didn't know if they were enough to make a life worth living, but I remained open to the possibility.*[10]

Amanda couldn't see two feet in front of her. But she was brave enough to take one small step.

What does a step toward Redemption Road look like?

For Cleopas and his companion, it was **welcoming a stranger into their home in the middle of their grief.**

For Puddleglum, it was **mustering the strength to stamp out a fire.**

10. Knox, Amanda. *Amanda Knox: The Life I Refused to Surrender*, 20 Mar. 2023, www.thefp.com/p/amanda-knox-the-life-i-refused-to.

For Amanda Knox, it was **doing sit-ups in her prison cell.**

For the dad in Mark 9, it was **trusting Jesus when everything in him did not trust Jesus.**

As I mentioned in the introduction of this book, my wife struggles with chronic fatigue. While we have gotten some answers over the past few months, there is still a lot of uncertainty ahead. Diana is a wonderful mother and gives everything she has to care for our son. There are days when I don't know how best to help her, and I feel so hopeless. There are times I am angry that God hasn't "fixed this" yet.

My cerebral palsy complicates the issue further because I can't take care of our son for long periods of time by myself. But you know what? There are things I *can* do, like give Diana short breaks throughout the day. It seems so small, but this is what a step toward Redemption Road looks like for me. And I know Jesus is with us in our struggles.

When my son Emmett gets frustrated that a toy isn't working, he looks at me and says, "Please Daddy, help! Please Daddy, help! Please Daddy, help!" Maybe I need to take a lesson from him.

Sometimes a step toward Redemption Road is simply

saying, "Jesus, help. I can't make it alone." And if that's all you have the strength to mutter, I have good news. That's the only invitation Jesus needs!

Doing the next right thing, even when we can't see what good it will do, is the final step toward hope. When we take a step toward redemption, we look up to find Hope Road in view.

💬 *Questions to Ponder:*

Have you ever considered that we wouldn't need hope if life were perfect? How has hope kept you going during a difficult time?

Why do you think Cleopas and his companion invited "the stranger" into their home? Does spending time with Jesus make you feel any differently? If so, in what way(s)?

What similarities do you see between Jesus' meal in Emmaus and the Last Supper (see Luke 22:14-19)? Why do you think their eyes were opened and they recognized Jesus at this moment?

Why do you think it's so hard to see Jesus during times of suffering? Have you ever had an "eye-opening moment" and realized Jesus was with you even though it didn't feel like it?

What are some ways you can live like the story of Jesus is true even when it doesn't *feel* true?

What does one small step toward Redemption Road look like for you?

Before moving on to the final stop, take some time to think about where you are in life right now. Where do you find yourself stuck or hopeless? Talk to Jesus about what doing the next right thing might look like in your situation. Ask him to give you the courage to do it. And, if you feel comfortable, share it with a friend. Things become less scary when we talk about them!

Stop 5:
Hope Road

Bible Reading: Luke 24:32-53
Supporting Passage: Acts 12:1-19

*"Didn't we **feel on fire** as he conversed with us on the road, as he opened up the Scriptures for us?"*

Wipe the sweat off your brow and take a look behind you. We have stumbled our way through brokenness, disappointment, and suffering. We have dared to take a small step toward redemption. And, looking back, we've realized Jesus has been walking the trail with us the whole time. Now, finally, we find ourselves on Hope Road!

But before we continue on, we need to stop and ask an important question.

What exactly *is* hope?

Maybe we should have asked this question at the beginning of our journey. But then again, it's a question we can only answer at the end. (I know that sounds like some kind of *Alice in Wonderland* riddle, but I promise I'm going somewhere with this!)

The Problem With Hope

One modern definition of hope is "the feeling that what is wanted can be had."[11] If this is how we define hope, we're in big trouble. It turns the word *hope* into a synonym for *wish*. Everything hinges on getting our desired outcome in any given situation.

A version of this kind of hope also shows up in Christian settings. We sometimes treat God like he's our personal genie. If we stay on his good side, he will fulfill all our hopes (AKA, wishes). When our wishes aren't granted, we wonder where we went wrong. Hope has failed us.

If we go back to Disappointment Road, we'll see that this is the kind of hope the disciples had. They "had hoped that [Jesus] was the one who was going to redeem Israel" (v. 21). And they hoped he would accomplish this goal in a specific way—by using power and strength.

This wasn't a bad thing to hope for. They wanted God to rescue them from oppression. And their ancestors had clung to this hope over the centuries, which shows a deep commitment to God. Israel had been ruled by

---

11. Dictionary.com.

Assyria, Babylon, Greece, and now Rome. They longed for the moment when God would set them free. We'd hope for the same thing if we were in their shoes.

Many of our own hopes in life come out of good desires. But when reality doesn't match our desired outcome, we need a better kind of hope. A deeper kind of hope.

And that's exactly the kind of hope our friends in Emmaus received!

On the Road Again

When we last left Cleopas and his companion, Jesus had vanished before their eyes. I imagine them standing there, mouths gaping open in shock. Eventually, they regain their composure and stammer out these wonderful words:

They asked each other, "Were not our hearts burning within us while he talked with us on the road and opened the Scriptures to us?" (Luke 24:32, NIV)

I love the way the Phillips translation puts this verse:

"Weren't our hearts glowing while he was with us on the road, and when he made the scriptures so plain to us?"

This is their "We should have known!" moment. As they think back on their time with Jesus along the road, they remember how they felt. Their hearts had lit up like New Year's Eve in Times Square! They were filled with hope and wonder with Jesus by their side.

Now Jesus was gone, but the hope in their hearts still glowed. Jesus was alive. What do they do with this information? They go back to Jerusalem and tell their friends, of course!

Cleopas and his companion hit the road again with no time to lose. They travel another seven miles back to the place where the day had started out so dreary. They journey down the same road, but now it looks different. It has become Hope Road!

Can you imagine if someone saw them on both legs of the trip—first going *to* Emmaus and then coming *from* Emmaus?

Picture an ice cream stand located somewhere between Jerusalem and Emmaus. The man behind the counter sees two people walking down the road. Their backs are slumped, and their heads are hung low.

"Hey! Want some ice cream?!" he calls out.

But they walk by him without so much as a glance.

Then several hours later, he sees them again coming

from the opposite direction. Well, he *thinks* it's them. They look the same, but they act differently. This time, they are jumping and singing their way down the road.

They run over to the ice cream man and say, "We'll have two double scoops of chocolate chip mint, and make it snappy because we gotta get back to Jerusalem!"

They hand over a $20 bill and shout, "Keep the change!" as they skip off with their cones like little children.

"What happened to them?" asks the ice cream man, scratching his head.

Hope happened. But it wasn't the hope of good fortune or wishful thinking come true. No, it was better than that. It was the hope that comes from knowing Jesus is alive.

When they get back to Jerusalem, they can't wait to share the good news with their friends. But before they can get the words out, their friends have some news of their own:

There they found the Eleven and those with them, assembled together and saying, "It is true! The Lord has risen and has appeared to Simon." Then the two told what had happened on the way, and how Jesus was recognized by them when he broke the bread. (Luke 24:34–35, NIV)

Apparently, Jesus had a busy Sunday. The timeline is a bit unclear, but while these two disciples were away, Jesus also appeared to Simon (Peter). Everyone was in agreement. Jesus was dead, but now he is alive.

(And the women who went to the tomb earlier that morning are like, "Yeah... We told y'all...")

Joy filled this room where there was once weeping.

Hope Played On Repeat

In most Bibles, the story of the road to Emmaus "ends" here with verse 35. You will probably see a new header appear before the start of verse 36. This may cause us to stop reading and close our Bibles. But the story is not over yet!

As everyone in the room continues to chatter away, something amazing happens:

While they were still talking about this, Jesus himself stood among them and said to them, "Peace be with you." (Luke 24:36, NIV)

Jesus strikes again!

This is our perfect ending: Jesus' friends believe he is alive. And now he appears before their eyes. All's well that ends well, right?

Not quite.

They were startled and frightened, thinking they saw a ghost. He said to them, "Why are you troubled, and why do doubts rise in your minds? Look at my hands and my feet. It is I myself! Touch me and see; a ghost does not have flesh and bones, as you see I have." (Luke 24:37–39, NIV)

There are a couple of differing opinions on why Jesus was mistaken for "a ghost." Some commentators think the disciples were kept from recognizing Jesus, just as our two friends on the road were. So, gripped with fear, they thought this person who popped into the room was an apparition.

Another view is that they *did* recognize Jesus. But because Jesus was dead, they thought they were seeing his spirit. This same line of thinking happens again in Acts 12 when Peter is in prison. After an angel helps him escape, he shows up at a house where the other disciples are praying for him. When a servant girl informs them Peter is at the door, they refuse to believe it! They dismiss the idea and conclude, "It must be his angel" (Acts 12:15).

I agree with this latter view. This is why Jesus encourages them to touch him. He wants to convince them they are in the presence of his physical body—the same body that had been broken for them three days earlier.

This has some major irony!

Even as the disciples were celebrating that Jesus was alive, they had trouble believing he was... *alive.* And remember, Cleopas and his companion are in this "startled and frightened" group. They have trouble believing again, too!

So what does Jesus do? Does he throw up his hands in frustration? "Ugh! I can't keep doing this, guys. I'm out!"

No. He walks through the same steps he did on the road to Emmaus. He plays hope on repeat! New Testament professor Fred B. Craddock describes the similarities well:

Although much briefer than the Emmaus story, verses 36–43 have essentially the same form: the risen Christ appears, the disciples do not recognize him, they are scolded for doubting, food is shared, they respond in wonder and joy.[12]

It's easy to laugh at the disciples for this blunder. But I am so glad Luke included this scene. It means the journey to Hope Road is taken in baby steps. And that's okay. Jesus walks with us at our pace.

---

12. Craddock, Fred B. *Luke: Interpretation: A Bible Commentary for Teaching and Preaching.* Westminster John Knox Press, 2009. P. 289.

In some seasons of life, the hope in our hearts will overflow.

But in other seasons, we'll need a daily—maybe even hourly—reminder that Jesus is with us.

We need the song of hope to be played on repeat.

Invited Into a Bigger Story

After Jesus confirms to the disciples that he is, indeed, alive, he promises to send them the Holy Spirit soon. Then he blesses them and ascends into heaven. Luke ends this story (and his book) with these beautiful words:

Then they worshiped him and returned to Jerusalem with great joy. And they stayed continually at the temple, praising God. (Luke 24:52–53, NIV)

Hope, joy, and gratitude has replaced their fear.

And so, in the immortal words of Boyz II Men, we have come to the end of the road. But the question we posed at the beginning of this chapter remains: *If true hope is more than wishful thinking, then what is it?* What is this deeper hope our two friends found on the road to Emmaus?

When I first encountered this story, I thought I understood its message. Cleopas and his companion were sad because Jesus was dead. But then they find out Jesus is alive. So here's the moral:

When we are hoping for something, we just need to keep the faith. Eventually, we will get it.

Sign me up for that deal!

There's only one problem…

That is not what happens in this story!

In the end, the disciples do *not* get what they hoped for. They hoped Jesus would flex his power and overthrow the government. Instead, Jesus sends them the Holy Spirit so they can continue the work he started. The work of building God's kingdom on earth as it is in heaven (Matthew 6:10). This work won't be complete until Jesus returns, but it begins now.

God's kingdom flips our hopes and expectations upside down. It is built not by power but by sacrificial love. In many ways, the disciples' lives got *harder* after Jesus defeated death and rose from the grave. Over the coming years, they would face trials, persecution, and suffering. They carried their cross the way Jesus did. Many Christians sacrificed everything, including their lives (often dying gruesome deaths).

We don't know what happened to Cleopas and his companion after their encounter with Jesus. But my guess is they joined in the work of building God's kingdom. What kept them going when times got tough?

They knew they were part of a bigger story.

They knew no matter how much pain they went through, Jesus was alive and by their side, enduring it with them.

This is the deeper kind of hope you and I need.

We need the hope of knowing we are invited into a bigger story. A story that doesn't hinge on whether or not we get all our wishes fulfilled.

It's a story that says we live in a broken world where disappointment and suffering are real. But it's also a story that says redemption is possible because God chose to enter into our brokenness. Because of Jesus' sacrifice, we are free to love and serve others the way he did.

As we go forth in love, the weight of the world's mess will still overwhelm us. The weight of our mess will still grieve us. Most days, we'll wonder if the small steps we take matter at all.

But the journey down Hope Road is a reminder that

they do! Because someday, King Jesus will be back to establish his kingdom on earth. And when that day comes, all will be set right.

I'll say it again. This, my friend, is the kind of hope we need!

Walking Hope Road with Jesus is not about getting our own personal happily ever after.

It's better than that.

Walking Hope Road with Jesus means participating *with him* in the greatest happily ever after of all time.

 Questions to Ponder:

Hope can have many different meanings. What are some definitions of hope you've encountered throughout life? How would you define hope?

Have you ever tried to stay on God's "good side" to get something from him? What was the outcome?

Has your attitude or mood ever changed after spending a little bit of time with Jesus?

Why do you think the disciples had trouble believing

Jesus was alive even when they knew it to be true? (See verses 37–39 for reference.) Is there any area of your life where you need to be intentional about playing hope "on repeat"?

What is the difference between the "wishful thinking" kind of hope and the deeper hope our friends found on the road to Emmaus?

How has Jesus invited you into his bigger story? What small steps can you take to continue building God's kingdom?

As you finish your journey, take some time to reflect on the roads you traveled: Broken, Disappointment, Suffering, Redemption, and Hope. What are one or two things you've learned along the way? How can you remember these things the next time you need hope?

And last but not least... Do you know anyone who needs hope? If so, invite them to walk with Jesus down the rocky terrain of Hope Road... And take the journey with them!

Conclusion:
The Perfect Travel Companion

Thank you for traveling down Hope Road with me, friend. As we end, there are two things I'd like to leave you with before we part ways.

First, please be gentle with yourself as you walk down Hope Road with Jesus. You may have finished this book, but that doesn't mean your journey is over. Take your time at each mile marker. You may still be on Disappointment Road or Suffering Road, and that is okay. You may need to linger on Redemption Road a while longer. There's no rush. The walk down Hope Road is not a race. Rest at each stop as long as you need to, knowing Jesus is with you.

The journey isn't always linear, either, as much as I'd like it to be. I wish you could read this book, reach Hope Road, and be done with it! But that's not how it works. Today you may be on Hope Road. If you are, you should soak it in. But tomorrow, you may wake up and find yourself back on Disappointment Road. That's okay. It doesn't mean you haven't made progress. It just means you need Jesus to walk with you every day. So be as patient with yourself as Jesus is with you. *He loves you!*

Second, as I close this book, I am reminded of a passage from the last book of the Bible. In Revelation 5, John is given a vision of the heavenly throne room. God is seated on the throne with a scroll in his hand. This scroll must be opened to begin the final plan of setting the world right. But there's one little problem: No one is worthy enough to open the scroll. And so John begins weeping bitterly.

John weeps because all hope is lost. The world is doomed to remain a mess unless someone opens that scroll. He knows he isn't worthy enough to open it. We aren't, either. We can't manufacture hope from within ourselves.

But then John gets some good news:

But one of the twenty-four elders said to me, "Stop weeping! Look, the Lion of the tribe of Judah, the heir to David's throne, has won the victory. He is worthy to open the scroll and its seven seals." Then I saw a Lamb that looked as if it had been slaughtered, but it was now standing between the throne and the four living beings and among the twenty-four elders. (Revelation 5:5–6, NLT)

John is told to look at a Lion. But when he turns around,

68

his eyes gaze at a slaughtered Lamb. This Lamb is worthy to open the scroll because he has suffered. This Lamb brings us hope because he has been battered and broken. This Lamb, of course, is Jesus—the one who walks Hope Road with us.

Everyone in the throne room begins to worship the Lamb with these words:

You are worthy to take the scroll
*   and break its seals and open it.*
For you were slaughtered, and your blood has ransomed people
for God
*   from every tribe and language and people and nation.*
And you have caused them to become
*   a Kingdom of priests for our God.*
*   And they will reign on the earth.* (v. 9–10, NLT)

As NT Wright explains, "From this moment on, John, and we as his careful readers, are to understand that the victory won by the lion is accomplished through the sacrifice of the lamb, and in no other way."[13]

This is both the beauty and the scandal of the Gospel. Hope—true hope—is only possible because Jesus has entered into our suffering. He's the perfect travel companion because he understands the full human

---

13. Wright, N.T. *Revelation for Everyone*. Westminster John Knox Press, 2011.

experience. He is not some faraway, apathetic god in the clouds. He is with us in our sorrows:

For we do not have a high priest who is unable to empathize with our weaknesses, but we have one who has been tempted in every way, just as we are–yet he did not sin. (Hebrews 4:15, NLT)

Jesus knows pain. He knows disappointment. He knows anguish. And because of his sacrifice on the cross, Jesus is worthy to guide us from brokenness to hope.

I hope you've enjoyed *A Walk With Jesus Down Hope Road*. If you found it helpful and would like to read more books by me, I invite you to check out my *Nobody Left Out* devotional series. You can learn more about my books at **Books.NobodyLeftOut.net** or by using the QR code below:

Start Reading

Can We Stay In Touch?

The journey may be over, but we can still be friends! If you subscribe to my free **Nobody Left Out Newsletter,** you'll receive content from me on a regular basis.

The newsletter is where I share the content of new books I'm working on to get opinions and feedback. I'd love for you join us! And as a thank you for subscribing, you'll receive the first five days of my 40-day devotional *Nobody Left Out: Jesus Meets the Messes* for free.

You can subscribe at **NobodyLeftOut.net/Newsletter** or by using the QR code below:

A Small Favor...

Thank you so much for reading this short book. I would love to get your thoughts on how you liked it. It would mean a lot to me if you left an honest review on Amazon.

As you may know, Amazon reviews play an essential role in reaching other readers. They help people decide whether or not this book is right for them. Reviews also help me gain insight into the things I got right, and the areas I need to improve. I want to get better as a writer!

Based on your review, I'll continue tweaking this book's content.

Feel free to leave a review at **NobodyLeftOut.net/ReviewHopeBook** or by using the QR code below:

Thank you!

About The Author

Michael Murray is just a messy, broken guy trying to follow Jesus one step at a time. He was born with cerebral palsy, a disability that affects motor skills. Living life with CP has given Michael a unique perspective on God's grace and mercy. He writes books to share the good news that every single person matters to Jesus.

Michael and his wife Diana live in Orlando, Florida, with their son Emmett and dog Ruby. (Diana is an amazing artist!) He is a big fan of sweet tea, musicals, and writing about himself in the third person.

Connect with Michael:

Website: NobodyLeftOut.net
Books: Books.NobodyLeftOut.net
Facebook: Facebook.com/NobodyLeftOut

Made in the USA
Columbia, SC
28 October 2023

25109004R00050